My Feelings

WHEN I FEEL
SCARED

Amy Beattie

E | **Enslow Publishing**
101 W. 23rd Street
Suite 240
New York, NY 10011
USA

enslow.com

Published in 2020 by Enslow Publishing, LLC
101 W. 23rd Street, Suite 240, New York, NY 10011

Copyright © 2020 by Enslow Publishing, LLC.

Library of Congress Cataloging-in-Publication Data

Names: Beattie, Amy, author.
Title: When I feel scared / Amy Beattie.
Description: New York : Enslow Publishing, 2020. | Series: My feelings |
  Includes bibliographical references and index. | Audience: Grades K–2.
Identifiers: LCCN 2019007735| ISBN 9781978511743 (library bound) | ISBN
  9781978511712 (pbk.) | ISBN 9781978511729 (6 pack)
Subjects: LCSH: Fear in children—Juvenile literature. | Fear—Juvenile
  literature.
Classification: LCC BF723.F4 B43 2020 | DDC 155.4/1246—dc23
LC record available at https://lccn.loc.gov/2019007735

Printed in the United States of America

To Our Readers: We have done our best to make sure all websites in this book were active and appropriate when we went to press. However, the author and the publisher have no control over and assume no liability for the material available on those websites or on any websites they may link to. Any comments or suggestions can be sent by email to customerservice@enslow.com.

Photo Credits: Cover Yuliya Evstratenko/Shutterstock.com; cover, p. 1 (emoji) Cosmic_Design/Shutterstock.com; pp. 4, 5 Rawpixel.com/Shutterstock.com; pp. 6, 7 StockImageFactory.com/Shutterstock.com; pp. 8, 11 blue jean images/ Getty Images; p. 9 Cavan Images/Getty; p. 10 Rat007/Shutterstock.com; pp. 12, 14, 15 Africa Studio/Shutterstock .com; p. 13 michaeljung/Shutterstock.com; pp. 16, 17, 18, 19 LightField Studios/Shutterstock.com; pp. 20, 21 Raygun/ Cultura/Getty Images; pp. 22, 23 AJP/Shutterstock.com.

Contents

I feel scared on Halloween. There are many kids I do not know. They wear scary costumes.

I go trick-or-treating with my friends. Some of our parents come, too. We have fun together!

I feel scared when I watch a scary movie with my brother. I do not like ghosts!

Then I remember it is just a story. It is like playing make-believe. The ghosts are not real!

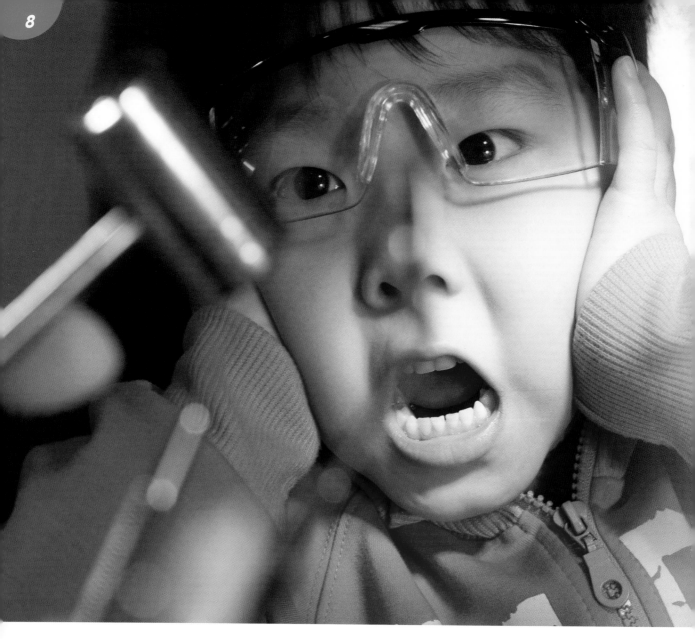

I feel scared when I go to the **dentist**.

The dentist uses sharp tools on teeth. What if it hurts?

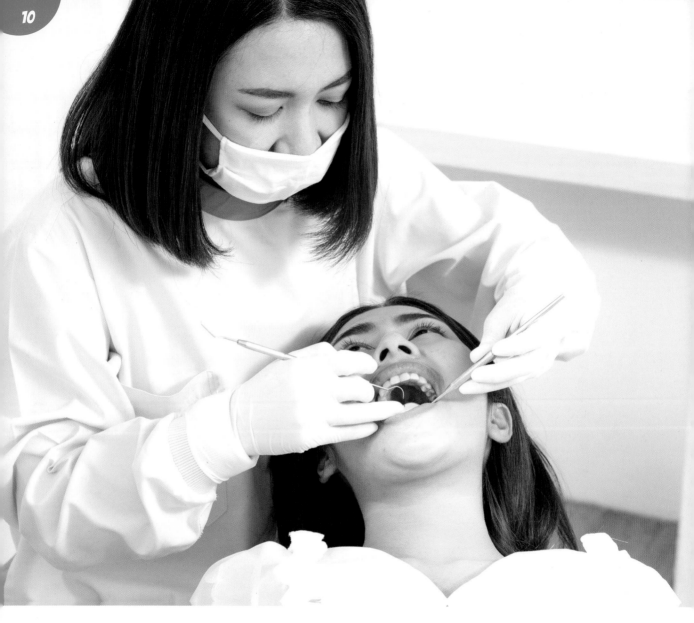

My mommy goes first. The dentist explains how each tool helps her clean Mommy's teeth. Now it is my turn.

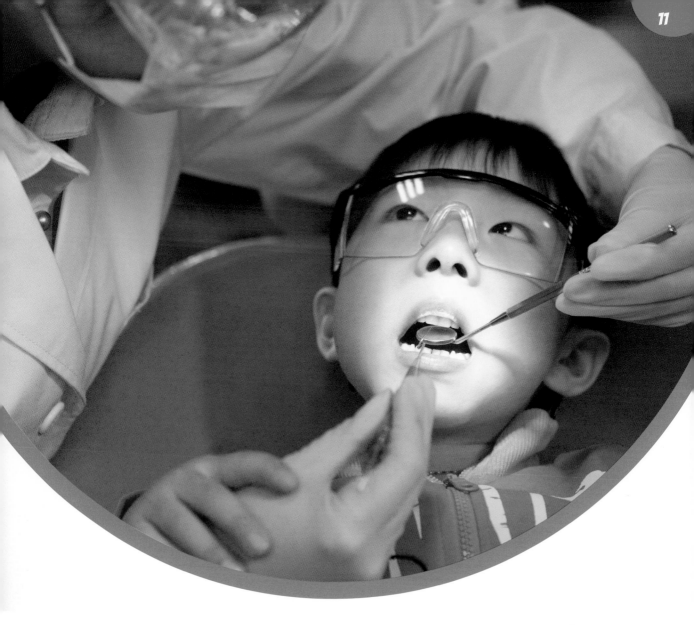

I hold Mommy's hand. I open my mouth for
the dentist. The tools are sharp, but they don't
hurt me.

I feel scared when my aunt gets sick.

The doctor takes good care of her. But the medicine needs time to help her feel better.

My little cousins come to stay with us. Sometimes they are scared. I decide to draw with them to cheer them up.

My aunt is **proud** when I help my cousins.

I feel scared when I ride the school bus. I walked to my old school.

I do not know the other kids. What if they are mean to me?

The bus driver is friendly. He asks my **neighbor** to be my buddy.

She says I can sit with her. Maybe I will have fun on the bus!

I feel scared when I fall off my bike. I cut my leg.

My mom checks on me. She cleans the cut.
I get back on my bike.

Scary things can happen at home and far away.

When we are with the people we love, nothing is scary.

Words to Know

dentist A doctor who cleans and fixes people's teeth.

neighbor Someone who lives near you.

proud Feeling good about something you or someone else did.

Index